A HAGIOGRAPHY OF HEAVEN
AND VICINITY

A Hagiography of Heaven and Vicinity

Michael Joyce

Broadstone

Library of Congress Control Number 2017954071

ISBN 978-1-937968-38-0

Design & Typesetting by Larry W. Moore

Cover artwork by Wassily Kandinsky,
"Allerheiligen II" ("All Saints II")
Used by permission of
Städtische Galerie im Lenbachhause and Kunstbau München

Broadstone Books
An Imprint of
Broadstone Media LLC
418 Ann Street
Frankfort, KY 40601-1929
BroadstoneBooks.com

Dann denke an das Leben selbst. Erinnere dich, daß die Menschen viele und bauschige Gebärden und unglaublich große Worte haben. Wenn sie nur eine Weile so ruhig und reich waren, wie die schönen Heiligen des Marco Basaiti, müßtest du auch hinter ihnen die Landschaft finden, die ihnen gemeinsam ist.

Then think about life itself. Remember that people have many, puffed-up gestures and unbelievably grand words. If only they spent a little time being as rich and peaceful as the beautiful saints of Marco Basaiti, then you would be able to find behind them too the landscape they have in common.

Rainer Maria Rilke:
Notes on the Melody of Things, VI

CONTENTS

PART ONE: LIVES OF THE SAINTS

LETTER OF PAUL

Waiting midst the phantasmagoria for the appropriate word
Saul of Tarsus comes to the shopping mall, a Chinese man
offers him a morsel of sesame chicken in a furled paper cup
from a tray of same, the people of god come into communion
although still in exile, and thus they give each other no sign
save the occasional exchange of passing glances, half-smiles.
Still impatient for the final days even after all these centuries
our reluctant hero nonetheless recognizes the end of prophecy
in this placeless place, and wearily sits alone at a plastic table
to study the variety of God's creation and the ways of man.
He's wrong of course, we've been through all of this before,
know the clichés so well we could sing them, for variation
we prefer the beach, domed stomachs laved with sunscreen
plump packages in bikini bottoms, toddlers, grandmothers
dressed like gladiolus, asymmetrical starfish missing limbs,
single lengths of razor clams, open books strewn on the sand
the whole Darwinian menagerie and underneath a constant
scent of lust, baby oil and oysters, seaweed, blood and semen,
beneath the screaming glee and wave rhythm a low moaning
thrums along the strand as couples press against the blankets
they have brought here for this purpose, the deferral of desire
no different than its articulation, salvation and damnation mixed.

PROPHECY ON REQUEST

That all the world will come to speak two tongues is no news,
Rome knew as much, likewise that the master loses his dominance
insofar as the servant knows not just what but how it is he thinks.
Cowering in an inner parlor from centurion or artillery she pulls
the veil more closely round her face and bites the hem to keep from
crying out while in the corner of the room the laptop goes to sleep
the milky light fleeing back from whence it came, some day she
will go to Hollywood and tell Angelina Jolie what she thinks, there
among the great white letters she will gaze down through the mist
to where the freeways slither like a nest of shimmering snakes
just inland from the lozenge of the endless ocean, they will speak
girls on a picnic eating dates and fried fish behind a bombed farm
outside Aleppo, long skirts flowing as they run along the ridge.
How different they will be then, hugging like schoolgirls or sisters
each of them knowing she cannot know exactly what the other does
and freed finally by that knowledge ascend then to unknown stars

Lives of the Saints (1)

sitting waiting listening watching a gerundial life
passing intransitive, in French what is it that passes
or again: what is it who himself did this, what's up
what's happening, qu'est-ce qui s'est passé, Quidditas
given personality, is our fate exactly, no one cares
for your philosophy, more things dreamt, dreaming
wanting being (seeming he knows not, the young
orphan) the Dominicans sending Thomas away
lest his mother, the Countess, distract him, lost him
nonetheless to his brother's army and Rocca Secca,
the dry rock from which two years after he descends
in a basket, intervening temptations only memories
ripe flanks of the seductress illumed by the torch
red lips shrieking, tamping her breasts in panic
where the flames licked them, a shame the Lives
of the Saints have passed out of favor, lush stuff
for an action game, a first person shooter perhaps
Quest for the White Girdle (contra concupiscence
mere mise en scene, polygons and texture maps
vixen's flesh splashed upon the donjon wall!
spectacular effect as the dove bursts into flame!),
all in all real playability until, that is, the university,
a kind of dead end, starting up again with Landulph,
Count of Aquino; Theodora, Countess of Teano.
real medieval feel to the music, upbeat anime tempo
under the title scroll, maybe begin with demons
attacking in a kind of dream, a locust plague,
ravenous birds on the plain near Monte Cassino.

THE LIVES OF THE ARTISTS

The lives of the artists are laden with pain
at least as it is reported in popular magazines
more irony already than he might have wanted
finding himself once again minor in comparison.
Perhaps one shouldn't read so much, or read
so much into what others are said to accomplish
living on a back road in Connecticut, drinking tea
on a grey day after walking the dog through the woods.

That is the life, he might have thought once
in a life long before this, caught up in romance
and remove before really knowing either.
Yet whether he knows them now still in question
and, while a good subject for serious artwork, not
one he is capable of addressing in any new way.

He would like to think there is more to this story
the account of a winter's day and the way the table
is laid out with a postcard of a Caravaggio painting
and a chrome Disney figure next to a plate of cookies.
All we have left of the brawler Merisi Leoni's careful
portrait ten years after his death, that and this postcard
and of course Ashbery's long poem among other scraps
memories of afternoons in foreign galleries, what was
the lira worth then and where was the museum with
the fantastic chocolate cake and perfect crema?

St. Thomas

A devotee of all there is to know, mornings the books strewn
mark the hours he has spent with your unread library, the table
sometimes piled with them as if a reconnaissance, this day
just two splayed there face down on the coffee table, a collection
of fiction and Derrida on escape. And now he is sleeping through
the long morning stretching toward the meridian and coffee
and the slow afternoon before his exploration can begin again.

Justus of Leiden paints Aquinas as a kindly Dutchman, slightly
porcine, dark eyes searching, black cap pulled down over his ears
it is as they say how you look at it, the so-called dumb-ox smiles
benignly, handsome jowls soft against the Benedictine cowl,
bemused by what the angels whisper as he mouths the gospels.
In most portraits he holds out the scripture before him but in one
famously cradles the maquette of an Italian Renaissance church,
gazing up past a bell tower fitted out like a Buck Rogers rocket ship.

His Travels That January

οὐδὲν ἀκιδνότερον γαῖα τρέφει ἀνθρώποιο,
πάντων ὅσσα τε γαῖαν ἔπι πνείει τε καὶ ἕρπει
—Odyssey, Book XVIII, 130-131

I suppose he could have come upon his eventual gravesite without
knowing during that long January before he went from hermitage to
the monastery, slid from the ambulance gurney onto the ICU bed, a
creature girded like a coppery, ancient sturgeon lurking indecipherably
just offshore along a serpentine, underwater stream bed before
heading into the dark trench that stretches south of Long Point on
Lake Erie near where in 1909 the tri-masted brigantine *Straubenzie*
sank in the silt.

That month all that held him down was himself, not yet strapped to
the diving bell with its choking respirator tube and angry electronics
nor yet on constant display under the twenty-four hour light as if a
memento mori for all still able to drink freely, swallow, recite lines
from Yeats, or laugh aloud. Surely over those weeks he'd driven by the
Main Street gate of Forest Lawn at least twice weekly in the Jetta on
his way from teaching to pick her up after her shift at Buffalo General
where two months later they would page her to get over from the OR
stat after he crashed, then as a professional courtesy leaving it up to
her to say finally when to stop CPR and declare her sailor lost.

He didn't often go for walks, although it is not entirely out of the
question that he might have left the faculty tower in the company of
some young poet during the unseasonably warm patch from the tenth
to fourteenth that month (though he wouldn't have felt well enough
to walk during the last warm spell from the twenty-eighth to when
he sank); he and the poet going out with coffee in hand and deep in
conversation, their steps taking them at the latter's bidding into the
cemetery parkland and eventually down the gentle hillside past the
awful fiberglass winged sculpture to where he couldn't have guessed
she would bury him later on among prominent and protestant citizens,
an unthinkable destination for South Buffalo Irish-Catholics from the
working class, a subject perhaps something he and the poet might have
touched on that day, in the midst of talk of Kyoto, the Bhagavad Gita or
Elisaveta Bagryana.

That the dead are capable of moving in our memories like mechanical figures in a diorama clock can't make them live again, no matter how lifelike the detail of this awkward, aquiline fellow with Keats' flowing hair—he himself, like his young protégée, also a poet—walking out uncertainly among the stones before attempting to lay out a section of the *Times* to sit upon, spreading it upon the dull grass of the same slight hillock where he would eventually rest, for these weeks though rest not coming easily, one shirttail escaping from the sweater, knee turning damp where the grass seeps through the day-before's business section, smoothing it with his free hand and motioning the androgynous poet to sit, coffee meanwhile splashing over the wrist of his other hand and dappling the newsprint brown, our Arlecchino paying no mind all the while to his and the world's dishabille, the harlequin and chaste inamorata still talking non-stop.

LIVES OF THE SAINTS (2)

The merest events unsettle, houseguests en route twelve hours away
a misplaced shirt, an idea for making a table from a driftwood plank;
over against them simple things, the new doctor who knows Caravaggio,
the smell in the air recalling an autumn road in San Costanzo.
More or less crazy moment to moment, obsessively hunting
the shirt up and down the stairs three straight times within minutes,
certain it will not reappear for months if at all, mad saints seek Jesus
with less fervor. "En Italie," the language learning programs say,
repeating it, "en vacance en Italie," it was so long ago and no
vacance, instead a retreat from the emptiness of August, a pilgrimage
to a whitewashed concrete terrace with a view of the sea.

Take me away, take me, the prayer of the virgins and martyrs
every small city with its own church altar pieces and portraits
all the same brown and crying for restoration, prendalo, prego
the African fellow trudging along the beach near Senigallia
selling scarves and trinkets from a bundle big as a camel's hump
shrinking to a dot then disappearing further along the strand

Where is the shirt, what should we have in the house for them,
how will he know whether the plank is strong enough to hold.

MAILMAN

Being God's postman is no fun, yaar.
Butbutbut: God isn't in this picture.
God knows whose postman I've been.
(The Satanic Verses, *Salman Rushdie*)

Life, by and large,
is good for him
he thinks,
the suburban street empty
in morning sun,
one sole car passing.
He will complete
his route and go home
to someone,
there will be coffee
and the television,
certain aches
gaining
of course, a daughter
maimed
with piercings,
the afternoon going on,
sunlight dimming,
a meal, a beer, more
television
pond frozen
into a blue lozenge
and before long the bed
beckoning,
some warmth perhaps within
another morning
to come

A life given over
to others' expectations
never knowing any
outcomes,
even the nakedness

of postcards
illusory, as if seeing
the improbable silhouette
of an ice skater
within a kitchen window
the postcards fluttering
in his fingers
as he draws them
from the sack
a magician
pulling doves
from a silk hatbox

Each day in passing
he weighs how much
is knowable,
what songs
play within this house
for instance,
melody lost
as a vacuum groans
back and forth
upon a faded green carpet.
Daydreams harried
by a conglomerate squawk
the black arpeggios of crows
in bare trees
lavender shadow
of noon
looming
over the scene.

No mere witness
he has his questions,
the source of our violence,
for example,

or what are the uses
that wonder,
unlike, say, arithmetic
is put to?
Though it hurts to think such things
alone and unable
to talk through the confusion,
yet no other place on any day
is more conducive than this
square upon square
the bare geometries
of lawn and driveway,
sidewalk and syllogism
in procession.

In time he begins to imagine
himself in some other place,
not running away from
a truly good thing
but as if some other he
walked beside him
through this labyrinth,
a blurred figure
in an out of focus photograph

MATINS

the temptation to begin each time with the fact of morning
monks shivering under the heavy wool of the white robes
or the Jesuit who explained the obscure vow of the pilgrim
why he thanks the Marriot and its employ for sheltering him,
the homes we have transient despite the real estate bubble
wealth portable, Armenian gift rug for the wedding couple
for example, domestic space when it is unrolled in diaspora
serving as both headrest and lap blanket during the journey
which is marriage, such dimensions begging no explication
as the sleepers head off alone to wherever it is they are going
fortunate she whose eyes close simultaneously with her lover
unlucky the one who studies the other's eyelids in darkness
as if seeing a great ship slide off from its dock in a newsreel
silent creatures waving from the wharf, the ballroom within
already glittering. O lord of little things, O king of sparrows
look after us, their weary prayer arises from the darkness,
hooded baritones chanting Te Deum in a univocal dawning
captions held aloft by angels in pre-renaissance scenes
all life unfolding in a flat single panel, birth to deathbed
motion studies of Muybridge, plump infant giving way
to youth, adult, and ancient in an implicate, pictorial arc

Sunday Morning

May some resounding rise over us we pray in whispers,
surreptitious, study one another on a bus, gazing off
through the window when the glance is noticed, yawn
ostentatiously to signal a general disinterest, contemplate
our own hands, hatch marked, plumpish, sagging, vaguely
saintly, the virgin's hand upon the shoulder of Elizabeth
carved in walnut by the Master of Constance, Baptizer
leaping in the dowager cousin's womb. Meanwhile scenes
flash by as if unreal, a small park behind a gilded fence,
a small boy in armor on a bicycle, the shadow of a man
surpassing him, if the sun were suddenly covered over
by an eagle wing would there be time enough to debark
before apocalypse? Is anyone listening as the driver sings
the names of avenues, whose heart bangs within its cage,
must all who traverse this world suffer? Foolish questions
pass the time between stops, none of this will be recalled
afterward, outside history, beyond memory, quotidian
consciousness loops like a gas station towel unwinding
from the dark and back up into it again, even clean linen
soiled by the memory of what has been, the human stain
pedestrian finally, furtive, the pristine white tiled room
an illusion, corners filthy where the mop does not reach,
citrus smell of industrial soap only half-masking decay.
God save us from the edges of things, recesses beneath
concrete underpass, bundles of greasy rags within which
homeless dream beaches and sauterne, fruit of the vine,
work of human hands unlikely to save us from anything
but us, this pilgrim's progress unrelenting and mundane
yet all we have of passing glory and thus duly celebrated.

LINES BACK TO JANE

Thank god
for the dreams they let me have, say all
his little subjects. Hold yourself.
All the things are moving in their containers.
Eventually, this will fail.
(Jane Gregory)

what is this distance between having and making

a point, love, a table upon which sits an uneven compass

the form of a wine spill, lips of the creature at the edge of the map

whence comes the tempest, is she a goddess? a child? made or had

what of himself, herself, made what that is, the ego, placement

a dancer, even in a chair, would understand, the point precisely

where one sits which isn't one exactly, but not (yet) bi- or tripartite

syllogism of the self (or is it dialectic?) the Vienna doctor baffled by her

willfulness, a navigator's brass protractor on the table between them

orb of the disk riding free along the arm of the station pointer

a parody of gender, Sakhmet breathing into the Pharoah's nostrils etc

who is in control of whom or what uncertain by degrees

Newcastle, Galway

I make of this suburb my own little island, rounding
the square of it, rain lashing in against my rented window from the west
whilst east of here is my own Pale, my black pool
wherein I look to see myself among the assembled undergraduates
a wintry June in this misnamed summer school, walking where my son
       did once perhaps
or even longer ago (who can know) the father of my great-grandfather,
though the chances are we've got it all wrong
that it was she who came from a line of kings, Mary Burke
via deBurgo and not the chieftain Thomas, whom my father's father,
each of them themselves Thomases, told my mother about:
the line of the eldest going back to the start, viz. Thomas de Jorse–later
       Joys.
But where'd that get you, Mr J? she may have thought, before naming me
       Michael,
to the consternation of her father-in-law with his one note litany of saints.
I remember him in his cream wool suit, silver hair combed back along
       the sides and across the crown
looking time in the face of the gold railroad watch cradled in the broad
       paddle of his palm

IDIR EATARTHU   THE BETWIXT AND BETWEEN

The things you see that make no sense except as themselves
a girl of twenty-something twirling a furled orange umbrella in the sun
the way the Corrib gathers itself above the weir
as if taking a breath before it tumbles on its run to the sea
the tallow corpse of poor Paddy's sister laid out at Clare Chapel, Galway
surrounded by the forlorn, hungry eyes of her relation
earnestly seated there around the white square of the stucco room.
Outside the caramel light of a summer even lingers,
night lying far off still this day of the year, out beyond the waves
that caress the shores of Hy-breasail, the isle of the blessed,
there where the black troughs surge and slacken
arise the silver seahorses and chariots in a faint glimmer
driving toward the cliffs where the choughs roost
then further still toward the low mounds and inland clefts
already in shadow now, already stirring

His Theology

He concludes, if that phrase for the moment may suffice, that there is,
if there is a God, a god for everyone, his brother who sees god as an
     accomplice
to the perfect cup of coffee, sugared like a Turk and with too much
     Half&Half,
a bantering grandfather type, prone to forgiveness; a god as well for
     the two stalwart lads,
one plump, one wan and vaguely nerdish, beating out the rhythm of
     Steve Reich's
Music for 18 Musicians for a full fifty of the fifty-five minutes of the piece
facing each other, two mallets in each hand, across the two xylophones
with no sign that their arms were growing heavy yet also with none of
     the ecstasy
of the pretty young soprano twisting in black hose and short skirt in
     her black folding chair,
her swaying form like a negative of (surely such a god will remember
     the age of the photograph)
Bernini's *Transverberation of St. Teresa*, the long dart of gold with its little
     fire at the end
thrusting through her heart until it reached her very entrails, so utter
     the sweetness, said the saint,
"that there was no wanting it to stop, nor any contenting the soul with
     less than God."

What comes and goes with less intensity also has its place in his theology,
     the leap
of undue optimism that nonetheless warms the heart after a glass of
     Vosne-Romanée
he thinks shows itself, as the liturgy has it, the fruit of the vine and the
     work of human hands;
a Vicodin can sans blasphemy have similar effect, a moment of unlonging
     eudaemonia
as near to prayer or its answer as we have any right to expect of our
     incarnation.
Likewise in seeing the lights within a house at dusk along a rural
     Connecticut road

we envision a sort of god in the faint surge of joy that for no reason
      accompanies it.
"I wouldn't use the term 'a god'," Derrida said of Heidegger, "but if the
      statement means
that we're awaiting the arrival of an unpredictable one, and that we must
      be hospitable
to the coming of this one, then I've got no objection."

Afterward, though, it is still Sunday morning and the riverkeepers are
      arriving for a potluck brunch
at the desanctified yellow and brown church of a neighbor, the children
      gathering in the street
gaze up at the tower to see how the clapper meets the bell at its mouth,
      tongue having polished the spot
to a sheen that a metaphysical poet might argue is the face of god. In
      another, literal coincidence
he whose gathering this is sat next to us at the concert last night, the
      xylophones lulling his date to sleep,
there being no accounting for how one or another woman responds to
      rhythms. Emily Dickinson,
for instance, tangled with the explanation of a bell whose slow tolling
      made a prison of heaven
opting for a more insistent good news. But it's another poem of hers
      that would have won these kids over,
the one that counsels "Split the Lark and you'll find the Music, Bulb
      after Bulb, in Silver rolled"
though dead birds are hard to come by even in winter, the finches
      clinging upside down on the thistle sack
like lively fruit, the White-winged Crossbill, the Common Redpoll,
      even the Purple jostling for the black seed.

THE RESURRECTION OF SOCRATES

Think of Socrates had he lived and Xanthippe
along the marble streets of Athens in sunlight
paying a morning visit to the lean young man
Lamprocles and his lover, let us call her Kypris,
the older man still full of expectation, awkward
in the company of women, looks downward
into the pool in the courtyard and sees her face
they are early and would have walked the quarter
for a time had she not appeared and ushered them in.
The young man emerges, scent of sleep still on him,
rubbing his face with a cloth, wine is poured, the two
women make desultory talk, sun floods the chamber,
it is a good thing to have lived the old man thinks
although he cannot quite follow what anyone is saying.
He has questions still of course but they are less generous
than once, more inward looking in the way a path winds
through silver flanks of olive trees within the sacred groves
to where the gods recline in the dying light, blinking when
a mortal happens upon them or a dew-brindled fawn

Saints in Sunlight

> "Maybe I am not very human - what I wanted to do
> was to paint sunlight on the side of a house."
> (Edwin Hopper)

Seeking a word against the pall which lingers
in the blue shadows of the woods that lay beyond
the pale, illumined porch, white rails and baluster,
white trim, clapboard, casing, even the bead board
ceiling white, yet all faintly tinged the milk blue
varix of an oyster, Beausoleil, say, or Bedeque Bay
skirts layered in stony ruffles, or on another porch
that day, demi-douzaine of Wellfleets *in* Wellfleet
crushed wedge of lemon gleaming in the sunlight
and the thumbnail of auburn cat's eye that remains
once the flesh and liquor is drained, pulsing rays
of honey light from the glass of fumé blanc waver
and reflect upon the bare tabletop. What spell or
charm, what amulet, will hold off the dark, where
do these ideas come from? the gall beneath sweet
barely perceptible, or how sometimes just to begin
to contemplate having to make sense of things turns
your stomach, vertigo rising in a whiff of turpentine.

The emptiness of seven a.m. you made your subject
a picture of the mind, afraid of itself, its possibilities
manifest, dull lavender crevices, dawn like a grey caul
peeled off, how the edge of a great lens is ground down
to make it opaque and gather in what light there is;
hating the sandpaper feel of it cupped in your hand
a hard-shelled creature nonetheless gleaming there
slipping the thing back into its purple velvet sack,
tightening the cincture, and going out in the morning.
At low tide a gang of rakers would arrive at the flat
where the barge had settled with the tide, filling it
as best they could with the jagged shells, hands
cracking with the seep of salt and iodine, pores
chalky, the Malpeques gasping in their baskets.

It is not the sea, he thinks, that seeks resurrection
or not as one thing, no solitary consciousness, rather
all that it collects within one inadequate category—
we could just as well call this dawn— the pure longing
for differentiation unrequited, instead the way the sun
laves the rills of a dental molding, flattens scrollwork,
traces a single hour across the planks of the floor
then retreats, giving way to whatever is the aftermath
of light, this suffusing something we find ourselves
within, not frame or framework, god forbid, illusion
perhaps, the unbounded boundness of being here.

THE LAWS OF PHYSICS

Times the laws of physics seem rescinded, toast not warming
despite the glowing coils within the apparatus, men soaring
down from towers on a bright autumn morning, mythology
conceivable then contra the beery smelling traders laughing
before Twombly's Leda, four guys out on the town late Friday
at the museum. *Jesus, they call this art*, not a prayer exactly
yet possessing the same potentiality if carried off, into dreams
for instance, or the unseasonably warm streets among tourists
and pre-theatre crowds, or when gliding between warm thighs
in the bed of a provincial goddess. Note how the building spins
upon its axis when you gaze down upon the atrium, Satan
smiling familiarly at your side. *All this*, he need not complete
the sentence. How you posed gazing at Matisse's dancers
in the stairwell so the girl in thrall there might feel simpatico,
auditioning lovers in each gallery or while drinking wine alone.
Weightless then as well, no inferno able to brand your soul,
no gaudy nightscape fully contain your visions of dominion;
at half your age you might have joined the young financiers
painted the town, danced on light poles, skulked back mute
to a sleeping wife on the last train home head still spinning

WASTING AWAY

Wasting away the late morning sun with lovemaking
left with the grey aftermath of empty early afternoon
breakfast dishes washed and put away, second latte gone,
Saturday paper bereft of news, no neighbors ever call,
few friends, the children grown, no taste for shopping
hours away from dinner and wine, no ready remedy
this malady without a name, anomie the technical term
acedia another, "the monk's disgust for his place in life"
according to the review. Eloise to Abelard unyielding
after all's said and done, "come not, write not, think not"
this much true of anyone, saints or lovers, poet, priest
rain against the tin roof of the hermit's Kentucky shack
room choked with cedar smoke from the stuck flue,
downstairs the steam iron huffs as she presses scraps
of Japanese indigo for a fugal quilt, a variation upon
Roman Stripe in whose dark diamonds light flickers
miraculously, small segments taking flight like wrens
from the nestbox, *Troglodytes troglodytes*, aptly named
older than us, here all year, abundant, mostly unnoticed.
"So then what? Nothing. Trees, hills, rain," the hermit
wrote to someone after his deepest disappointment,
bound by obedience to remain within this world.

KARL WALLENDA ASCENDS INTO HEAVEN

(He shouted "Hold Tight!" NYT 3/22/78)

Karl Wallenda
on the wire between hotels
in Puerto Rico
his knees bent
against a wind he knew
would not end
waited calmly
to feel himself go over
holding on to
the long pole and
the last instant
then falling
like Icarus.

We would like to believe
this accomplishment itself
was pleasing.
To have lived a life
as a man who
married, worked
fathered children
and saw their children
your shoulders
supporting a pyramid
carrying and then mounting
the cross
endowing the modesty
of your possibilities
with a patriarch's death
transpired above
other men.

But we know nothing
his apostles, the remnant,
the flying weary

fallen angels
ourselves still
carefully dancing
on the shifting cable
of a world beneath.

LAST WILL AND TESTAMENT

Perhaps he should have texted this,
the message opening at once
upon a hundred screens,
seen by the two or three
who have an interest
in terminal musings,
Terpsichore having become
invisible again,
sound waves dancing
between towers on distant hills
still sheathed with fog.
Live on,
live on, the message
would say
perhaps ambiguously,
pronunciation
difficult to parse
under the circumstances.
Who are these dancers
in diaphanous white skirts,
and why do they cling
to the resting earth?

A Prayer (1)

let some simple word come
set aside pronoun, the story,
decorative description, names
tell exactly how it is here now
attend without expectation
although giving rein to desire
this moment will still elude

the sun shines down evenly
in such seasons, shadows only
an interruption of the light
a strict geometry governing
festivals and movement
torpor in the place of wind

white stones line the garden
here to there and back again
shrubs regain their fragrance
bitter, dark berries forming
a child keeps counting to ten

.

A Prayer (2)

Beyond the station
the light lies in wait
gathered over the winter
in these white fields
it explodes the grey
and is too much to look on
we beg spring to take it away

NOTE TO THE ABSENT FATHER

"we where sad when you left
    but now your back"

the hand of him who wrote this note to the absent father
(thus a prayer) was firm, holding off what he could not imagine
and so accompanied with guignols at each line break, grotesque
smiley faces alternating with frowning ones, leering
circles marking the abyss within which a child cannot speak
nor could the father ever confess what he did not know of it
before subtracting one from the circle of the four of them
on the lawn in the sun outside the yellow house the car rumbling
off to some version of the future, none then able to see beyond
their own rendering of the masks, frown only a smile upside down.

Two decades later the note yellows on the board where it was left
pinned like a drab moth, marking hopes that the ordinariness would
lapse, divorce divorced of its ennui, the boy the man had been
no longer looking for some conventional sign of happiness, or not
at least in the comings and goings of a world that cannot put away
the relics of a hope that love would outlast us, if not last forever.

THE PILGRIM

Leaving days before departure setting out shirts and socks
the little amber barrel with the pills, botanicals and nostrums
two cloth belts of contrasting colors for the genteel south,
the books and electronics, pens, the journal to write upon
or within, a question of orientation, this girding like every
he can remember since adolescence a rehearsal for death
where such questions take precedence, upon or within a life
not a matter of local usage but the perspective from which
one sees oneself, owl in the ruin, or how, the artist suggests,
as cell phone relays increasingly roost in church steeples
there is a growing risk of interference from hapless angels

Still we set off, or in stillness we find ourselves caught up
in an almost biblical sense of transportation, lifting off
like Saint Dunstan, his the most modest of the levitations
only an inch or two before his death, or the bin Ladens
heading homeward on their chartered jet in the lull days
of September, laden with Neiman Marcus bags and crates
of California avocados, the best in the world by their lights,
appalled that the errant nephew had so wrenched them
without warning from poolside, golf course and sauna
as outside the cabin windows falling creatures flapped
like absurd birds in search of the perfect sacrifice

Leave or leave off, the difference between them slight
how a butcher manages to slip from the rump roast
to the fat of his thumb, a thin section like a biopsy
not more than a burn really after a lifetime of this
calculation, its language that of theatre, how we will
stage this, in situ or metastasis, where are you going
in the company of this stranger and who will you be
when you get there, and how will you find your way
through the terminal to where the driver is waiting.

The Darkness

By this stage the darkness
becomes congenial, no less
replete with demon or abyss
making one's way across
the upstairs hallway, *la Chute*
or— how do you say?—*il tombe*
perhaps, how it will be,
what next act remains to us.
Falling like a starlet, Dietrich
or Judy Garland, the dark
both sexes and unsexes
binary in a way Dante knew
awaiting *Der Blaue Engel*
mesmerized by the heavenly
portal of her thighs. This waltz
with the devil a walkthrough
akin to prayer, holding on
to something that isn't there.

Increasingly sleepless whilst
episodes of panicked waking
pass, surfacing from a cave
beneath the water and lost
again to water, the dim room
dawning to itself once more
lately giving in, or over, to it
each night dying before it starts,
supine to decubitus, vice versa.
Meanwhile the muses dance
softly about the blue waters,
or so Hesiod reports, the last
in his catalogue of their praise
Oceanus and dark Night then the
deathless who surround them,
the holy race of those who are
for ever, though forever
what he wisely does not say.

In West Ham it's become a football
anthem, a chase for dreams that fade
and die, pretty bubbles in a cabaret
song long gone hooligan, astray on
shores of hope as shadows creep
knowing by dawn the bluebird
too will be gone. After the match
dark or dreams look alike under
ghost light, the darkened pitch,
still smelling of beer and sulphur,
skulls aching from the silence.

Dreaming both alone and not, still
solitary no matter that someone
shares our bed, having come full circle
and more aware than ever how daft
that phrase, adolescent sleeplessness
unlike late middle age, man and boy
differently, indifferently engaged,
restless each meaning something
else by it, like sisters, one doing one
seeing, equipoise of Dante's morning
dream: Leah in a meadow gathering
blossoms, Rachel rapt before her
looking glass, Feste singing
"Come away death" to a girl.
Some by eye and some by scent,
some via a proprioceptive fumbling
in the night, we make our way
there wherever we are going in the dark.

THE SAINT

Sees not
the self
in the mirror
there but
who one self
has been
just before
dying
eclipses the light
this instant
cannot extinguish

Part Two: desert dialogues

GOSPEL

My brother talks of his pain from the car in which his daughter
drives him on the day between scans to pick up wife and mother,
after work before they return home for a dinner of take-outs.
He will try, he says, to eat some of a sub sandwich, another brother
and his wife are coming over. "I am a little depressed," he says,
his voice strong nonetheless on the cellphone. It is not just
that the pain continues, but that he doesn't feel like himself.
"I remember Dad saying that was what he hated about his pain,
that he could not give back to the world." The simplicity of this
disclosure shocks me, and I feel a little envious, five days short
of twenty-six years after his death, that he shared this and not me.
However I do not envy the fraternity of pain linking father and
second eldest son, already a little afraid that I will not be able
to stand up to it, let alone sit still in a darkened car through wintry
streets, talking of how important it is to reach out to others, how
he will try to do more in coming days, how good this call has been.

Passarelle

In the morning mail writing from two women, a poem and essay,
one younger, one not as young, both Buddhist in nature, a dancer
and an architectural theorist, though neither so easily characterized,
Student and teacher, mother and daughter, though not to each other,
Aussie and Yank, Californian and Southern Sea, philosophers really
he thinks, embarrassed that he did not conceive of this at first

What links them, if anything, is the thin thread of his consciousness
a passarelle above the flood tide which he treads oblivious and earnest
from the basilica to the café where he orders a cichetti of crisp fish
as if the two of them were at the table with him, getting acquainted
in the way women do in the company of a clueless man

One has written an ode to a common object, the second a meditation
on the wind, in this they have much in common which has little to do
with him or the fact of their womanhood or where they are located
among the four corners of the known world or the Ages of Man
yet in this instance he thinks himself a conduit of circumstance
perhaps the only person likely to read both these texts

There is little mystery here although it can look like this at first
no course of action or close reading required, no confirmation asked
they are as they are and they have written to say this although not
entirely to him, nor for that matter solely to themselves

AN OLD VAUDEVILLIAN

I would say the same thing to my uncle, my dentist
says to me, he means I think—kindly—to avoid
saying I am as old as his father, meanwhile waitresses
now call me dear or honey, I have lost both menace
and allure, I think, father figure or worse
to the woman at the supermarket whom I cruise
I think discreetly and still receive the languid smile
that signals she's seen me, along with an expression
that instead can be read as saying you cannot be
serious, you seem a nice fellow, but try not to make
a fool of yourself. It is of course too late for that,
the countenances of each fool I've been are clay masks
I wear one upon another in a semblance of myself
protagonist now become comic figure, grimace
gone to dyspeptic leer, the homonymic king
taking a dance turn, shuffle ball chain on the heath
before a hovel as the stage directions go, O blow
winds blow and crack your cheeks, trala haha

A Gift (second poem for Gabriella)

Our history is queered, all relations questionable
and questioned, the "mother of us all" and the painter's
blurring, and she who is to come daughter of one or both
or, as in Asanga's Teaching of Great Compassion, all of us
mothered and mothering at once in the way the waters
mingle here above the dam near Upplandsmuseet where
the girls sit on the shore opposite, skirts spread to gather
the sun between their legs, laving it across the fretwork
of their birdlike chests as if a lotion of endless youth.

In the lie you lived on his account you saw this portrait
and yourself in it as clearly as the painter himself did
standing in the sun at the café along the Fyrisån
while you smoked your cigarette, talking of himself
with you become a variety of longing, which is your gift,
at least among the ancient men who carefully court you,
watching, O Iris Chrysopteron, you laugh and run off
slipping between the worlds we inhabit like dream,
iridescent seam between night and what is to come.

A MIRROR (FOR MICHAEL MCCARTHY)

Sometimes there is an older man in the mirror
other times a younger, his father or a lost brother
both of them wandering through time to this window
what life they have beyond it undecipherable
whether they converse as strangers in a station
or in some deeper dialogue conducted over years
building a mutual understanding albeit no answers

To call one of them Socrates a common gesture
making the other Euthyphro by allusive geometry,
how the story is told and how it comes down to us
the cocksure youth putting his own father on trial
mirrored by the philosopher's cross-examination
on the nature of piety, a word now out of fashion
not helped much by moral duty, the usual translation

If how we act depends upon the one looking in on us
then what we mean is arbitrary the old fellow argues
yet if the face in the glass loves us for what we do
it isn't his loving glance that makes us good, is it?
the two of them gaze out at him, beautiful and lost
bemused by the symmetry, the impossible burden
of such language, the hinge on a gate, a gold clasp
at a lover's soft throat which unveils the mystery

OF OBJECTS IN DREAMS

What is the status of objects in dreams, the papers spread
upon a counter in the background where someone works
yet with no role otherwise in what unfolds? Did these
play some part in this world once now lost in memory?
A shred of ribbon in the grass, an acorn along the path,
my brother sitting upon a low stool high in a meadow
just beyond the shade canopy of a venerable crabapple,
his face illumined and a red thing, scarf or flower
a blazon against the black suit and vest he wears;
leaning slightly over his spread knees, a single beam
shining on his great placid face, just he and the red thing
glowing there before the ash grey trunk and its filigree.
Meanwhile off-stage an apparatus limns a gaudy picture of
his fate in orange and violet: here the heart, these the lungs,
the dark beads where the lymph nodes lay no rosary
but instead the happenchance of fallen fruit, black rot
or flyspeck or where the worm burrows into sweetness.
And what of the wry smile of the man in the meadow?
Is that a thing among things or a state of being we call
dreams for wont of a machine to scan the mind's innards?
What if he emerges holding an acorn or eating an apple,
star of his own film, the follow-spot upon him still?

Nearness of Things

"despite all conquest of distances,
the nearness of things remains absent"
    –Heidegger

Bored finally by cleverness, enjambment, empty complication
how things gather in the back seat of the car, a map taken idly
from a tourist information kiosk, long-billed khaki sun cap,
polished peach whorl of the mollusk shell, faintly blue beneath
the broken labra, sand pitted, smooth, the rough plaid blanket
it ended up within, leaf grit and sand upon the floor mats,
wayward candy pellet, a single penny, a quarter, a brown glove.
The mind inventorying itself constantly, low persistent hum
of the dark lozenge inside its putty-colored carapace, hard drive
doing what it does to preserve itself. Your words make you
vaguely ill when you see them again like this, so obviously
needy, ornate and yet finally pedestrian, omnium-gatherum.
It would be quite a trick to bring all this to some conclusion,
provisional or propitious, the way things end finally illusive.

WAITING FOR NOTHING

The feeling of waiting for something when there is nothing,
revels neither ended nor scheduled, no bus rounding a corner
no front coming in, neither rising wind nor bud in blossom
yet still waiting in stillness and green expectation, looking
neither inward nor in some landscape or the gaudy precincts
of a city, but waiting with the vacant deliberation of desert
fathers, fallen into a nameless moment with no way to say.

How to wait this hour out when the next will be the same,
the question of pain or first love, the urgency of whatever
this moment cannot convey elsewhere otherwise remaining.

A flock of birds might now take wing and circle the trees
setting down again in the same place. A minister once
flew like this from Nashua to Exeter, New Hampshire
on a clear day without wind or kite, his frock coat hardly
billowing. A woman in a field near Hampstead reporting
the devil held the weeping man by his hand, though no
other witnesses are recorded, the churchman struck dumb
his eyes clouded by cataracts long before this miracle.

In a hotel room in Atlanta

The single early moan of the man beyond the wall
is unreadable as ecstasy, pain or merely waking
and does not stay in mind beyond this. He wants
to write on torture, an old friend says over dinner,
in many ways it seems the only subject given what
we have come to. A philosopher, he does not know
whether he has the courage to take himself through
tribunal accounts or the testimony of survivors.
Do they walk the earth, he wonders, as if new born
or blank eyed in a rictus of disbelief. A sad smile
crawls across his face like the outline of a river,
say the Snake where it turns just below Boise
like the leer of a jack o'lantern, jagged face carved
the dull knife lingering where the damp flesh spills
its expression frozen to something beyond wonder

Manichaean

The pause for an ancient sin slowing the unfolding day
coloring it in all the ways nuns illustrated with chalk
the soul like so, slowly filling as if with milk but do not
imagine this, think instead of it as rising blackness.
No apology to people of color necessary then, all of us
white, although our white likewise a gathering darkness.
Difficult notions for a photographer's son to account
the ghostly grimaces of the negatives in the enlarger
giving way underwater to an actual sea change, light
rolling into darkness, grimace metamorphosing to grin;
the reverse of this apparent in Spring along tornado alley
dark clouds gathering at the end of Washington Street
like a motorcycle gang, some with a sickly green pallor,
a few bright faces among the mob of Cumulonimbus.
Once gathered they began to march, Orangemen
to a Lambeg Drum, menace of the familiar worse
than a dark dream or vision of damnation intervening

SALVATION

The grime of going without bathing, feverish for days
green effluvia and the aching weight just lifting an arm;
if you want to be saved come forth now, but where?
The savior's skiff on the horizon resolves into a prow,
a few rude planks where he stands, stinking rope, fish entrails
along the hull and the loaves like stones in a graying basket,
the eyes of the apostles as weary as yours, parched lips, warts
festering sores, before being at sea they have walked for days
in deserts where the people came out like grubs from their huts
and he would stop for each, wiping their eyes, wasting the balm,
the serenity in his face merely some end stage of exhaustion,
finally uncertain whether they wanted to rest here or move on
they wheeze like pack animals at a brackish water hole.
Here is the miracle of persistence, do you like what you see?
No matter, there is an end to everything, camphire flowers
dried to wads of straw beneath his sandals, the widow's eyes
wide and white with fear when he daubs them with spit.
And now come ashore again from a breezeless voyage
salt upon tongue and nostril, children wailing at the fringe
where the crowd presses against them, wisdom out of question;
unless you become as these, he smiles, it is too much to ask.

A SEASON SPENT

A season spent intermittently moving among cooled boxes
a hell of sorts, the dull staring at the brume of bluish light
planning assignations for creatures of one's imagination
awaiting approval from somewhere for one's heroic plans
counting the delights, rereading one's own emails to others
then going over the aborted first pages of a treatise
on the present and how it presents itself differently to us,
writing to and for no one yet deserving no credit for that
much persistence, *L'alchemie du verbe* notwithstanding.
Elsewhere weary birds wheel in the sharp light, a few
falling to the earth out of lassitude, dark clumps sliding
from a burnished plow. Far off beneath a fading showbill
an acrobat totters on a stool, visages of angels and nymphs
both fading into dun, smudged where they've been pawed.
Empty man in an empty room going nowhere in the heat,
all the books unread and, for him, unreadable, who lacks
a soul in the way the fire of a candle lacks at its center
bright mandorla of nothingness surrounding the wick.

NOTHINGNESS OR PLENITUDE

Is it against the nothingness he works
or the plenitude he wonders, angels
descending each whisper a single word
he cannot parse, but nods devoutly as
they turn and climb up again, sandals
beneath silken skirts, rough ankles,
isn't it wonderful he thinks, the question
real but addressed to whom? like all
such questions unmarked but not
rhetorical since the latter supposes
an audience while he stands alone
by the base of a ladder in a vacant field
staring up into the brightness where
silver rungs converge as in perspective
drawings. Suddenly he wonders how
he sees all this without interference,
ethereal forms miraculously pellucid
although what holds the ladder up
for now at least he does not ponder.
This isn't a dream, he knows, nor some
extended metaphor for inspiration, hope,
or the nature of language. No, there are
angels, industrious and incomprehensible
creatures who labor to convey matters
of enduring importance to a population
mostly deaf. Still nothing troubles them,
perhaps the message they relay at bottom,
soi-disant choirs and heavenly chorus,
no more or less than this susurrus.

ALONG THE SILK ROUTE

All day the lapsed sacrifices compounded
water bought and left at the counter
another bottle later one had to ask after
then rearranging the fold-down altar
between him and the red-haired girl in coach,
a stranger, the shock as the plastic cup erupted
dark wine splattering like blood
upon his black checked shirt and jeans
a wound he felt sure she knew better than he.

What it means to be in transit
is to be without refreshment
even if it is offered
thus drink when you can and
do not count on much.

The gambler in the shuttle van
paid with a crisp fifty
from a discrete stack of bills
fastened with a rubber band
stacked in a hardsided caramel briefcase,
his eyes a little worse for wear, striped shirt
a wreck after a night stuck in Vegas
after Santa Barbara was socked in.
Now trying to get home the slow way
like hitting a back-door draw
or dowsing in a rocky field.

Here come the dromedaries
you can hear them snort and plod
miles away in the desert night
and the muffled thunder of tamped sand
shifting under their oafish hooves
the great beasts sighing under the weight
and the camel herders whispering.

We, too, have been chasing night all day
and finally now caught up with it
beginning our descent over the Great Lakes
another hour and a half of rocky air before us
dim mathematical roil of waves unseen
troubling the leaden sea on a moonless night.

Ab nihilo

From nothing nothing but the dawn
was once a pencil of uncertain light
viewed by the desert fathers perched
like buzzards on makeshift shelves
hovering above a cloud of nothingness
Wile E. Coyote speeding by in silence
running laps in the dim lavender dawn.
The world's a wind-up clock, the heart
a spring alongside two toothed cogs
which move the limbs in semaphore,
the Vitruvian man now trademarked
let's start anew a measure for what
can be, strip out the vein from groin
to aorta and in its place a copper tube
salt slush coursing straight to the eye,
cornea icy blue as an unnamed moon

THE ANGER

Deep within like a muscle ache although it starts more subtly
toward the surface of the skin, in the chest and face, spreading
to the tongue and lung at once, word and breath connected
by this raw, monosyllabic music. One wants to strike out at
something (all this exactly at such a remove, as if the event is
happening to someone else, an amiable fellow in a classic film
on a remote cable channel) Isn't it lovely to live here, someone
should say, but chemical reactions allow no retreat. All this too
ugly to relate, living as we do in the age after machines, two
epochs past that of animals, the bitch with her dog one has
swerved to miss in the night shouts "asshole" and slamming
the car into reverse we commence a perverse geometry of
insults, clamoring dominant-to-tonic by turns in the street
call and response still simmering afterward, lingering into
morning. What's done does not matter nor who lived happily
ever after, this moment grates, hate simmering in a thin soup
of bones and nettle as throat closing, we choke on our hymns

WHAT WE HAVE TO SAY

That we find what we have to say increasingly a chore
seems wrong to us but we do not know what else to do
forlorn and lost in the face of a history that bores even
its inventors as they face the microphones and cameras,
even in the bedroom no dreams but images called up
as if on the screens where we sit looking at each other
over laptops, their undercarriages warm upon the thighs.
Messages come and go, pictures of pretty things to buy
needs and desires a distinction made in listen & repeat
tutorials in foreign languages, coats of all sizes for sale
in various colors and fabrics, a wide array of choices
listed in ranks of categories, the living and the dead,
dull video of a girl on a webcam talking about her dad
and how she misses him, wearied by this insistent light
we check once more for news, look up at each other
then blink, rub our eyes, yawn and get ready to sleep

THE REMOVE

Silence of remove or its opposite the same
emptiness, the same fullness

who are you never
answered, boreal
owl, jewel
in the blue shadows
of the spruce

the wind shakes
the windows
a cousin consciousness
kenning and cunning
likewise
what we see through at issue

transparency and persistence
in the same root
green curve of the ergonomic trowel
from her daughter
slumber of rhizomes
sequence of Matisse's Blue Nudes
or how the iris sees through
the winter as well

dog star staggers
toward the solstice
contrite
principles of commutation and distribution
applying alike to the calculations of the heart
keeping himself from her
a way not to lose
himself in her or her from him

KENOSIS, OR THE EMPTYING

Along the trail in the Redwood forest he explains how it could have been
            otherwise, say
a fiercely possessive, vindictive god: low grass slashing like numberless
            knives, moss
smoldering, the loam searing underfoot, a constant assault of saplings
            bruises the flesh,
and trees pummel furtive bands of creation's refugees who move through
            the shadows
seeking surcease, but before whom reeking flowers spit, hiss, and close
            into cicatrices.

Instead nature is left to itself without any need of us who separate
            ourselves from the flea
or titmouse or the wafer of stone that tastes of salt from the spume.
            Meanwhile a friend
of my son gathers spruce berries to stud the roasted trout when in a
            meaner epoch he himself
might have been flayed and set out on the spit or under a sun that shrivels
            flesh into leather.
What mercy the shade is instead, the mist along this ridge, what grace
            the elk that dances
upon that ridge, the puma that stalks it for days, the creator who
            disinterestedly watches.

AN INCREASE OF CROWS
(for Belle Waring)

An increase of crows in town, I think one of them is my dead brother
and imagine there is an underlying code to their presence, like hex
or binary, things my father taught himself late in life to scant result,
an animated hexadecimal train moving silently across the screen.
Roman legions held similar beliefs about crows, which I find
are "short distance migrators" according to a website. I'd ask
"Brother what've you come to warn me about?" if only I understood
their tongue, the alternation of cawing and the high screech and whir
of the one—I think this one was him—flying low along River Street,
fleeing I suppose whatever it is that the shades flee in disguise.

THE SIMPLE POWER OF GRACE

We sit awaiting the snowstorm the day after Christmas
upon the same sofa where we sat last night, lost
in our individual thoughts. "What are you thinking?"
she asks but I can not reply beyond a thin smile,
caught by a clear memory of a particular intersection,
where Slottsgränd meets Kungsängsgatan in Uppsala,
the streetscape in sunlight but unlinked to any event,
just a place I have been at different times: on the way
to the supermarket, to the station and thence to Stockholm,
or to Systembaloget, the state liquor store, for Ripasso;
or the time we went looking for vintage black-tie regalia
stopping for sushi after none of the faded tailcoats fit.
None of this remarkable, save the vividness of the vision,
how it came to mind just after reading a meditation upon
the silence of god, and how happy it made me in aftermath,
the sense of an ordinary place upon this earth.

Acknowledgments

"Simple Power of Grace" was published in *AGNI* (online), 2012.

Cover detail from Wassily Kandinsky, Allerheiligen II Auch gennant, "Komposition mit Heligen," 1911, used with permission of the Städtische Galerie im Lenbachhause and Kunstbau München

Thanks to all the folks at Broadstone and especially Larry Moore, with whom, as Wendell Berry wrote, "it came clear: /the world that has tried us and showed us its joy/was our bond."

Of all the angels and saints who fill my life, none more than Carolyn.

About the Author

Michael Joyce once thought to become a Jesuit and perhaps became one nonetheless (his own father once described himself as "Jesuitical, self-taught"). He is the author of thirteen books spanning a career as a novelist, poet, critic and theorist, digital literature pioneer, and collaborative multimedia artist. His poems have appeared in *Agni*, *Beloit Poetry Journal*, *FENCE*, *FOLLY* (LA), *Gastronomica*, *The Iowa Review*, *New Letters*, *nor/*, *Notre Dame Review*, *Parthenon West*, *Spoon River Review*, *New Review*, *OR* (Otis Review), *TAG Journal*, *The Common*, and *THE SHOp* (Cork). With Gabriella Frykhamn he has published translations of the Swedish modernist poet Karin Boye in *Spoon River Review*, *Metamorphoses*, and *Notre Dame Review*. Two book-length sequences of poems, *Paris Views* (2012), and *Biennial* (2015), were published by BlazeVOX [Books]. He lives along the Hudson River near Poughkeepsie where he is Professor of English at Vassar College.